I Love you
Gramma Nana

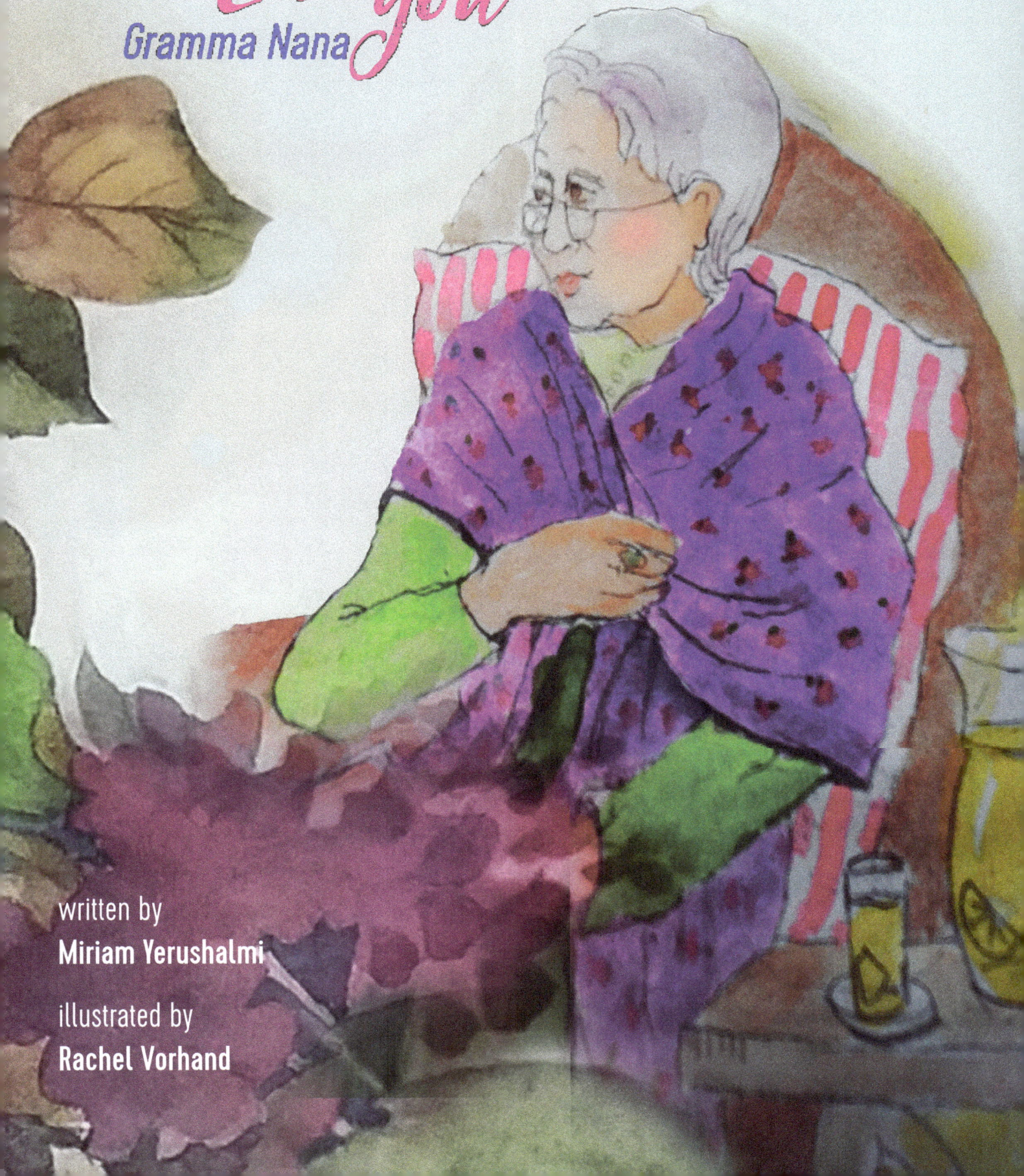

written by
Miriam Yerushalmi

illustrated by
Rachel Vorhand

IN LOVING MEMORY OF MY GRANDMOTHERS:
Esther Levy
&
Flor Varda Korkidi

SPECIAL THANKS TO:

Jason Zaiderman & family
for their help in funding my projects

Rachel Vorhand
for her beautiful illustrations

Nechama Dina Laber
for publishing my projects

Breindy Oelbuam
for graphic design

Reva Baer
for editing

I Love You Gramma Nana

ISBN 978-0-578-44232-7

This book is dedicated to the memory of Wanda B. Goines, whose rendition of her poem "The Gift Wrap and the Jewel" touched me so deeply. Her beautifully thought out words of timeless wisdom, delivered with such grace and soul, inspired me to give the grandmas in my life a portion of the recognition they so richly deserve for all they do and all they are. I resolved to create a book for grandmothers and their grandchildren to share, to read to each other while enjoying each other's company. I hoped that such a book would also inspire grandmas to make the most of their special position and to view the time spent with their grandchildren in the most positive way.

When I was approaching a milestone birthday, I fortunately came across a video of the Lubavitcher Rebbe teaching particularly that as we get older, we should increase our efforts to accomplish our mission of changing the world for the better, because there is only so much time left. Research shows that the number one factor to a long and healthy life is being active and staying involved. Grandmas, I hope this book helps you to realize your own value, and inspires you to do even more today than yesterday, as best you can in your unique way suited for your unique stage! We need you!

My mother-in-law, Leah bas Avraham, was an active person all her life. She worked full time as a nurse until the age of 88, yet she was always there for her children and her grandchildren, and always fully involved with their joys and concerns. She was adored by her family and is greatly missed.

So, to every Grandma, Bubby, Savta, Jadda, Grand-mère, Oma, Babushka, Nana, Nonna, Nai Nai, Wai Po, Maa Maa, Po Po, Abuela, Babcia, Giagiá, Avó, Mhamó, Nagymama, Bibi, Mormor, Farmor, Fafa, O baachan, Tutu, Kuku wahine, Halmoni… May this book bring you a fraction of all the joy, love, and warmth that you have brought into our lives! G-d bless you grandmas of the world!

Excerpts from Wanda B. Goines' poems used with the kind permission of her family.

For Grandma a new stage in life has just begun
Life has been passing too quickly for her always with much yet
to be done

She certainly had a gifted way
Of making the most of every day
Somehow she always knew
How to make you smile as you grew

"Good morning" she would welcome you with cheer
Oh how she loves you, was so very clear
She tickled you from head to toe
Until your face was aglow

She took you here and there and to so many places
What happiness was written across your faces

She tried so hard to bring you joy
Even buying you so many toys

Today after years have gone by
You look at Grandma
And what do you see
But a little lady next to you.
With wrinkles and wispy white hair
And you ask yourself
How did she get there?

You're looking at the gift wrap and not the jewel inside,
A living gem, and precious, of unimagined worth,
Unique and true, your special Grandma, one of a kind on earth.

And you may ask for now, what can I do?
Visiting her is a start for everything she did for you
My dear it's clear without any trace of a doubt
That we ought to help her now
Because that is what love is all about

But what limited time we have had
If you think like that you could get really sad
But of course we must not!
Cause every moment counts a lot

Let us try to keep her spirits high
And remind her how much she means to you
Maybe she hasn't got a clue
You think 'But how?' Alas!
What shall I say?
How should I be?
You can tell her in all honesty
"Grandma you mean the world to me"

Tell her how grateful you feel
For all those years she dedicated to you
It really was a big deal
Tell her again and again
"Grandma for years you had such a knack
For setting things on the right track"

I luv u
Grandma

I luv u
Grandma

I luv u
Grandma

I luv u Grandma

Grandma

I luv u

I luv u Grandma

Grandma

I luv u

Grandma

Grandma

I luv u

I luv u Grandma

I luv u Grandma

Grandma

I luv u

I luv u Grandma

I luv u Grandma

Grandma

In vibrant tones that impart
The feelings of your heart,
You know the pretty nice words that chimes like bells
Arranged in a way that clearly spells
Your attitude of gratitude

I luv u
Grandma

I luv u
Grandma

I luv u
Grandma

I luv u
Grandma

I luv u
Grandma

I luv u
Grandma

I luv u
Grandma

I luv u
Grandma

I luv u
Grandma

I luv u
Grandma

I luv u
Grandma

I luv u
Grandma

I luv u
Grandma

I luv u
Grandma

I luv u
Grandma

With words both comforting and wise
And with a twinkle in your eyes
When things don't appear to be the best, help her cope
And give her hope

So, it's really a matter of being there for her, you see,
That will bring her contentment daily

Smile to her like you already know
Even just a call with your sweet hello

We got to get busy
Fill up her days with positivity
To add flavor and spice
To make her day really really nice

It means so much to say I love you a lot

Please give it all you got!

Bless her for strength and health

With every ounce of your breath

Blessings for many years to come

Tell her again and again and then some

Grandma there is no one like you!

And then she will bless you back again and again for all that you do!

So remember dear children!
Look at the jewel inside,
A living gem, of unimagined worth,
Unique and true, your special Grandma, one of a kind on earth.

Thank G-d you have a Grandma!

IN LOVING MEMORY OF
LEAH BAS AVRAHAM

<u>LEGACY</u>

Tears have been wept down from my face

Grandma grandma where are you now?

I could see your holy face your image in my mind

All our beautiful memories are forever mine

She worked and toiled to fulfill her goal

Let heaven and above bless her soul

A true grandmother that was what portrayed

Self-sacrifice is what she clearly laid

The woman who fought for what was right

A full-time nurse way into the night

She is loving she is caring to this very day

Grandma you always remain in my heart

The thoughtful lessons which you pointed out

I will carry your legacy on

We will carry your legacy on!

My daughter was 12 years old when she composed this song for her grandmother.

MORE BOOKS BY MIRIAM YERUSHALMI

CHILDREN'S BOOKS

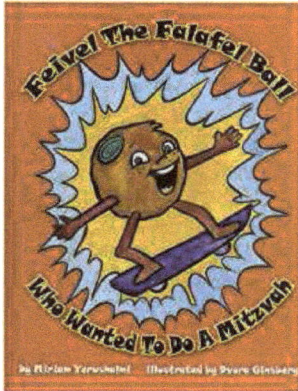
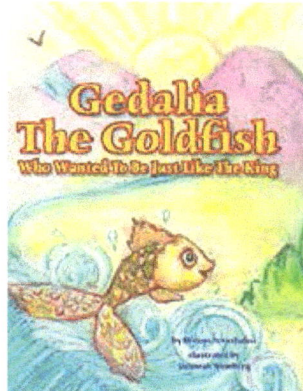
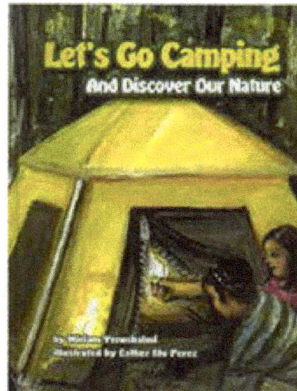
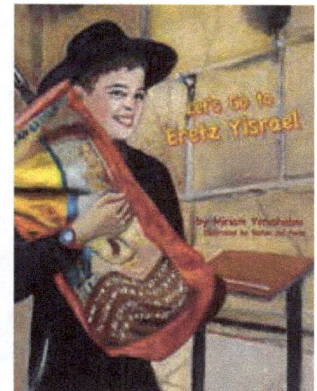

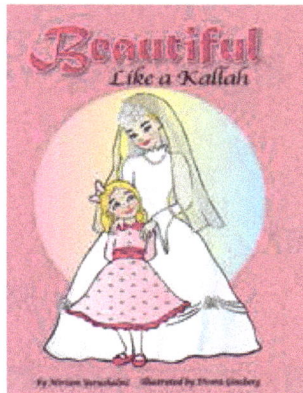
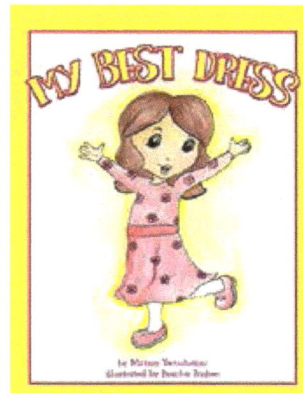
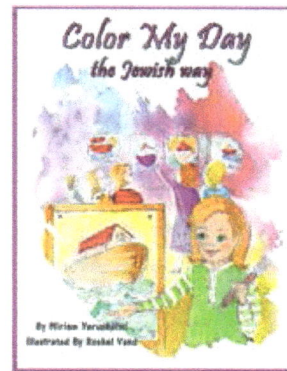

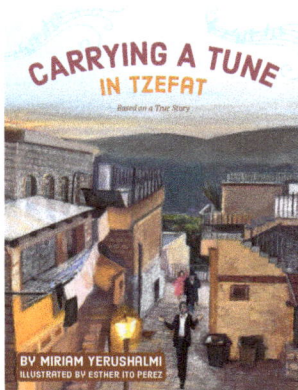
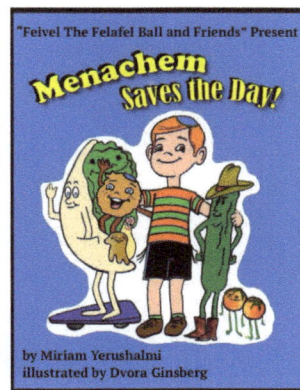

COMING SOON:
- Rainbow Fun Foods in Wonderland
- Yehuda Gets Fit
- Gedalia the Goldfish Helps Chaim Become a True Prince

ADULT BOOKS

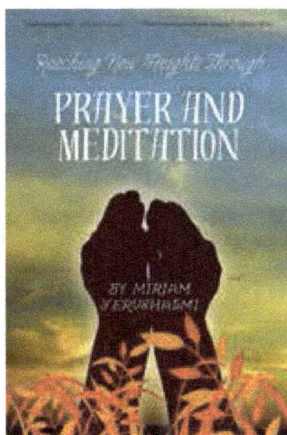
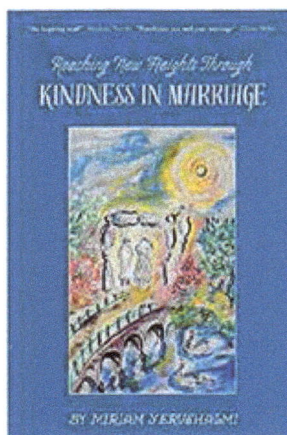
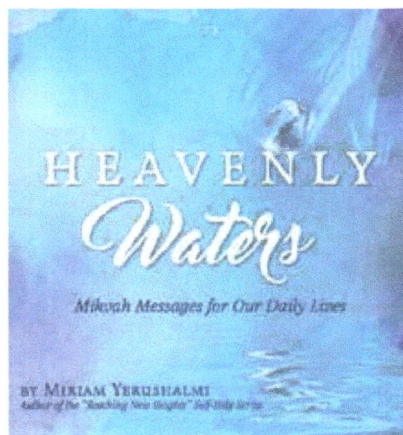

COMING SOON:
- Castle Around my Heart
- Reaching New Heights Through Inner Peace, Health & Happiness

AVAILABLE ON AMAZON.COM

www.ingramcontent.com/pod-product-compliance
Lightning Source LLC
Chambersburg PA
CBHW040303100426
42811CB00011B/1347